BEING SMART WITH MONEY

A PRACTICAL GUIDE TO THINK & RECONSIDER YOUR RELATIONSHIP AND INTERACTION WITH *MONEY*

CYNTHIA JOHNSON
Certified Financial Coach

Published by Lee's Press and Publishing Company
www.LeesPress.net

A Premiere Self-Publishing
Services Company

All scriptures are from the Bible Gateway KJV

ISBN-13: 978-1-964234-07-6

PAPERBACK

TABLE OF CONTENTS

ACKNOWLEDGEMENTS

I thank God for the opportunity to write this book. Special thanks to Mrs. Erica Jett, the CEO of the Empowerment Palace Firm for helping me birth this book into reality and encouraging me, holding me accountable, and walking with me through this process.

I acknowledge my parents and life experiences that played a major role in preparing me to write this book.

INTRODUCTION

Living in financial bondage, under the weight of debt can steal your joy, peace, freedom, and financial independence. The stress of financial debt and lack of money management can also rob you of your health and disrupt relationships.

I am not a fan of debt, and I believe the greatest financial goal is to become debt free and effectively manage finances. Money is a tool and as with any tool, if used inappropriately, it can cause harm, damage, consequences, and regret.

This book was written to share information that will challenge you to think and reconsider your relationship and interaction with money; get clarity and understanding as to what is at the core of your negative financial habits, behaviors, and decisions. Are you ready to start your journey on being smart with money? Then I invite you to journey with me through this book.

MY STORY

My financial journey started when I was in college and had numerous credit cards. I was young and lacked discipline regarding finances. I knew and understood the concept because my father taught me the principles of paying bills on time, managing money, budgeting, and saving. However, I chose to do it my way.

Years of doing it my way landed me in an unhappy place financially. It was stressful, and I knew I had to do something.

The card offers would come in the mail, and I would sign and accept and off I went to spend and enjoy the moment. I must admit I paid my bills on time. I just had a lot of debt. I had the technique of paying bills down to a science. I knew the due date and the closing date for each statement. Therefore, I would juggle the two.

If I wanted to make a credit card purchase and didn't have the money, I would wait until after the closing date to make the purchase. This would allow me time to get the money for the next payment. Making a purchase after the closing date would mean the charge would not show on the current statement, but the next. This would allow me time get money for the payment due.

This went on for a while. During this time of this financial madness, the Pastor at the church I attended in Jacksonville, Florida emphasized debt freedom and not being in bondage to debt. If you have ever been in debt, you know it feels like a heavy weight resting on you. It will weigh you down emotionally, physically, and spiritually. I was getting tired of the circus act (juggling bills).

It was then I had a "aha" moment, and I realized that I no longer wanted to live bound to debt and under its thumb. I was ready to take control of my finances to promote a positive lifestyle change. I made a decision and a commitment to myself to do the required work to defeat debt.

I began reading about credit history and credit scores to get a clear understanding of how I needed to position myself to promote a positive lifestyle change. It was then that I began to do the work. I realized that I needed an accountability partner and someone to help me devise a financial plan to get out of debt. In other words, I needed someone to oversee my financial zz accountable. So, I did.

As I reflect, I realized this person could be titled as a Financial Coach although that was not his title. I'm very thankful for my moment of transparency and vulnerability to own up to my financial madness (debt) and do something about it. It was an embarrassing and difficult time, but I'm glad about the journey. I did the work and promised myself I would never allow my finances to control me. While on the journey to financial freedom, I learned about debt consolidation, interest rates, fees, negotiating, and understanding credit. I acquired a better understanding about interest rates, fees, credit, and the true meaning of wealth. This required time, discipline, and commitment, but I didn't give up.

The hardest reality during this journey was realizing that money is tight when paying your way out of debt because all monies are allocated. I had to reduce expenses which was difficult. But sometimes we must make those hard decisions to reduce expenses that are not really a necessity.

I have given you a backstage ticket to My Story and

after you read all nine chapters, you will be positioned to change your perspective, behavior, habits, and your relationship with money. Are you ready to start the journey of being smart with money? As a Financial Coach, Licensed Real Estate Agent, Board Certified Credit Consultant, and member of the Credit Consultant Association, it is my passion to assist and support individuals who are READY to move from financial chaos to financial independence by taking control of their finances.

CHAPTER 1

DO YOU KNOW MONEY MATTERS?

It's Not About Having Lots of Money, It's Knowing How to Manage It!

Are you ready to get a handle on your life and money? In this chapter, let us step into a new realm on money and why it should matter to you. There are three important facts that will awaken you and your relationship with money.

Money Fact #1

Financial freedom should not be an option but a goal. The opposite of financial freedom is financial bondage and the lack thereof. In financial freedom, there are two ingredients you will need: responsibility and choices.

Responsibility is being accountable to self. I challenge you to make the ultimate decision to take control of your finances. Every change or transformation starts with a decision. It's never too late! So, let's start now the journey to financial freedom by deciding to take control of your finances and make healthy spending choices.

You ask, "How do I make health spending choices"? You start by identifying your wants versus your needs. This may be the most difficult task you will undertake, but it will be well worth it in the end. With every decision to make a purchase, ask yourself, is this a WANT or a NEED. Until we can take control of our finances, this is the method I recommend you use to develop healthy spending habits. Developing new habits takes time, consistency, and determination. Even if you miss the mark and make a mistake, forgive yourself and start again. Rise up and keep going!

Money Fact #2

Financial freedom also positions you with the power and authority to negotiate with lenders. When it is time to buy your first home, a car, or to start up your business, you must have a healthy relationship with money. Healthy spending habits yield healthy and strong credit scores, which most lenders use to determine a person's risk for credit or loan—something you may need if you want to make large purchases.

Strong scores help leverage your position when applying for credit or a loan. You have the power to negotiate costs, fees, and interest rates. Why pay more when you can pay less? That's exactly what a low credit score will get you. Paying more for your purchases. How do you pay more for purchases? You pay more because of the high interest rate. For instance, you make the required payment, and most of the payment goes to interest and then to the principle. The higher the interest rate, the more it will cost you. Stop giving away your hard-earned money by paying higher interest rates. Keep more money in your pocket by doing the work to become financially free.

One of the most important things you can do is to stop using credit for non-essential purchases. If possible, set goals to pay with cash. Of course, this takes time. However, while working to meet this goal, if you're going to use credit, I challenge you to use it and manage it wisely.

Money Fact #3

Financial freedom empowers familial relationships. How? Financial freedom positions families to relish in vacations, dining out, or a fun date night. Some families financially do not have the option to enjoy family vacations. The stress of financial chaos can rob a family of the simple pleasures and fulfillment of life. Positively changing your spending habits will yield positive results, causing less stress and more time to spend with family.

Financial freedom alleviates stress and sleepless nights. Financial chaos may often lead to health problems such as high blood pressure, anxiety, and depression. This stress often bleeds over into work performance, family interaction, negative thoughts, and sometimes low self-esteem. You must not live with the burden of being in bondage to debt. It is time to step into financial freedom so you can see your coins turn into real cash and have your money work for you.

Financial freedom is a result of effectively managing income and expenses, paying your bills/creditors timely, and investing in yourself by saving and/or investing. Paying bills on time is a huge factor to improving credit. Do you know that 35% of your credit score calculation is based on payment history? Paying your debts timely is a win/win.

You are developing and mastering healthy spending habits and at the same time, positioning yourself for financial freedom to take control of your finances for a positive lifestyle change. The word of God says that when we are faithful over a few things, He will make us ruler over many things (Matthew 25:21 King James Version).

My goal is to provide you with information and insight that will challenge your thinking and help position you to experience financial freedom, going from financial chaos to financial organization to promote a positive lifestyle change.

CHAPTER 2

YOUR RELATIONSHIP WITH MONEY

Now that we have discussed financial freedom, let's talk about your relationship with money. We all have a relationship with money; that relationship can be good or unhealthy. Prior to now, you may have never considered your relationship with money. As with any relationship, there are emotions, triggers, habits, thought patterns, and belief systems that we bring into the relationship between you and money.

This is probably an "aha" moment. A moment to reflect on how you and money have interacted. Now that you are aware that you have a relationship with money, let's go a step further to gain clarity. Please read and answer the questions below. These questions ca help you identify and get clarity regarding your relationship with money. Please write your answer to each question in the space provided.

- What emotions do you feel when you talk about money?

- What thoughts do you have when you think about money?

- Do you have obsessive thoughts when you interact with money?

- Do you have negative or positive thoughts when you interact with money?

- Do you interact positively or negatively with money?

Once you have answered the above questions, you may be asking yourself, *how did I form this type of relationship with money?* —especially if the relationship is not a good one. I will answer you with a question. Have you considered that your relationship with money was possibly formed without you even knowing it? Formed by your environment, bad habits, what you learned and experienced in life? Please afford me the opportunity to be honest and to say that I believe that sometimes what we learn, and our life experiences may not always produce positive results even with the relationship with money.

When finances are involved, this can lead to cycles of chasing more money, never having enough money, never getting out of debt, or never having control over finances. Healthy relationships are formed when you set boundaries, have a balanced perspective, are disciplined, committed, and determined. This is also true with money. This chapter is an opportunity to self-reflect and assess how you and money interact. As you take a moment to reflect; how do you rate your relationship with money? If you are having trouble rating yourself, allow me to help you get started, by answering the following questions:

- Do you overspend?
- Do you set financial boundaries/goals?
- Do you feel anxious when spending?
- Do you feel powerless over money?
- Do you feel that you have no control of your money and that money controls you?

If your rating is low, (meaning you have more negative responses than positive), we must help you understand why you and money may be fighting. Are you ready to stop fighting and be smart with money? Are you ready to get positive results between you and money and no longer allow money to control you? I challenge you to stop living under the weight of debt. It is time to break bad habits. It's time to take control. It is time to make a CHANGE!

Culture and Money

Culture and environment play an important role to how you may relate to money or interact with money. There are many factors that affect a person's ability to understand and effectively use various financial skills such as spending, saving, investing, managing money, and financial decision making. Culture is the biggest influencer. Let's begin by understanding how culture influences us, and how culture can impact our perception and relationship with money. Why? Because it plays a big part in your thought process, habits, and financial decisions.

What is culture? Culture refers to the shared beliefs, values, customs, behaviors, that characterize a group of people or society. For the purpose of this book, when I reference culture, I am referring to family. The definition of culture is very broad and encompasses a lot more than what I will share in this section. My goal is to share information that will help you understand the relationship between culture and your relationship with money.

It is within the family structure (culture) that we learn habits, behaviors, and our mindset (way of thinking, opinions, and attitudes) are established. Often times, the negative money habits, behaviors and wrong mindset can be traced back to our culture. Knowing a person's history can tell a lot about who they are and how he/she manages money. For example, if I grew up in a home where there was always a lack, there is a great possibility that as an adult, I may spend money excessively because I felt deprived and do not want to feel that again. This is one of the ways that culture can impact a person's relationship with money. Also, if my culture lacked financial literacy, it is more than likely I will lack the financial skills to use money wisely. If you have never had the opportunity to see money as a learning experience, you may feel overwhelmed talking about money and lack the understanding and skills to be smart with money. We imitate and learn from the people we regularly interact with. If you lack financial skills, I challenge you to decide to change and to begin developing your skills. The repeated cycles of mishandling money stops with YOU!

Chances are, if you don't learn good money habits, then you won't repeat good money habits. You repeat what you learn. As we continue to explore culture and how it influences your relationship with money, are you beginning to understand the connection between your culture and your relationship with money? Can you see how your fight with money may be due to the lack of positive financial influences and influencers?

Also, experiences within a culture help shape our belief system. For example, if I always experienced financial lack, I may believe this is the way it will always be, and I resolve to think that I can't do better or that I will never get out of debt.

Sometimes as adults, the negative spending habits, poor financial decisions may possibly be symptoms of something deeper such as low self-esteem, unhealthy relationship with money, lack of financial literacy. It is much easier to walk away than to fix the problem that lies deep within the individual.

If we can get to the core of the problem and acknowledge them, we can accept truth, cultivate a willingness to make changes, and heal. Moving away from negative thoughts, habits, and decisions to a place of positive and productive thoughts, habits, and decisions, helping us take control of our finances.

Too much of anything is not good. Too little of anything is not good. However, it is important to find a healthy balance in all things. I pose this question to you. Did your culture have a healthy balance or is your fight with money a result of a financial imbalance? When I speak of culture, I'm speaking of the environment and influences that you have been exposed to as it relates to finances. Maybe your culture was saving, maybe your culture was spending, maybe your culture did not have any organization with money, it was just money, or maybe there was always tension because there was never enough money.

To begin understanding why you may have recurring money problems, I challenge you to look back over the past years to reflect and to determine the kind of culture you were exposed to and how it has impacted your relationship with money.

Our experiences, whether good or bad, can become our belief system. What belief system did you develop because of what you experienced and learned as it relates to finances?

How was money managed in your household? Who was your financial role model? Based on your answer, is it time for a change?

Now that you have taken a moment to reflect, let's go a

little further. Identify key things that you recognize that were passed down (by habit, mindset, experience) to you or that you learned about money and about finances that is negative. Below are questions that can help you identify negative influences or recognize negative patterns. Please write your answer to each question in the space provided. Writing your answers will help you gain clarity.

- How do you view money?
- How did you culture influence your relationship with money?
- What do you believe about money? about money?
- What was your experience with money as a child?

Take a minute to assess your thoughts and beliefs about money. There is no right or wrong, just ways to improve our perception, and habits. With the questions above, were you able to identify negative behaviors, patterns, cycles, and what you learned and experienced and have carried into adulthood and possibly passed down to the next generation in your family? If the answer is yes, then it is time to make a change.

I think it is safe to say that change starts with identifying and acknowledging there is a problem and most importantly, deciding to do something about it. But how can I change when this is all that I know? I'm glad you asked. Any change starts with a renewed mind. A mind renewed with new information influences your thoughts, belief system, and behaviors. Renewing the mind is vital to initiating the process of change. Many of our beliefs about finances were developed during our childhood. If we weren't taught finances, we learned from the authoritarian family members. To change negative beliefs about money and how we handle money, it is important to renew the mind with new and positive information about money and develop new money habits.

We also bring into adulthood the money practices we witnessed and experienced within the home as a child, mimicking what we learned or experienced. If these practices were negative, then negative is what we take into adulthood. It is important to transform the mind with new information. Insanity is doing the same thing but expecting different results. If you don't like the result of something, then it is imperative to make a change.

Change occurs when our capacity for information increases. Change can be temporary or long-term. Long term change is when you decide to do the work and go through the process of renewing the mind, developing a new belief system, and practicing new habits. When we do the work, go through the process, the chances of reverting back to old habits are lessened. Let me say this right here, "there is no quick fix to taking control of your finances to promote a positive lifestyle change." The options are trim excess spending and prioritize by budgeting or increase household income. You can also pray for a miracle, but if you haven't gone through the process to deal with the core issues of money problems, then you may find yourself repeating those unhealthy habits and cycles.

Three major areas of growth that will help you have a better relationship with money are:

- Respecting money

- Change your mindset with money

- Change your behavior with money.

An example would be, I can win one million dollars, but if I do not have a healthy relationship with money, I will spend it and have nothing to show for it. Habits and what you practice do not change if the mind doesn't change or is renewed.

Renew the mind + make changes = get different results.

Spending Habits

Let's talk about types of spending habits. Habits are formed by repeated behavioral patterns. Behaviors most often repeated are the behaviors most likely to form into habits. The same is true with spending habits.

Ask yourself, "What kind of spender am I?" I think it is safe to say that all of us fall into a type of category based on our spending habits. Here are a few to think about:

Signs of an Emotional Spender

Emotional Spender is a person who spends money during a time when your emotions are heightened. This is a time when your emotions have taken control of all your power to reason, and you operate out of an emotional state. We may tend to buy items we really don't need and may not even want. Emotional spending is often used as a coping mechanism to help soothe internal pain, provide temporary feelings of gratitude or satisfaction, and build a false sense of self-esteem. Do you know that jealousy is also identified as emotional spending? Yes, it is! It is part of how we may feel about ourselves. Society pressures and seduces us to compare ourselves and what we have in measurement of our peers, affecting our self-esteem, and as a result, we spend to keep up with our peers. When what we really need is inner healing and peace.

Here is a list of a few examples of triggers that may lead to emotional spending (fear, grief, sadness, jealousy, and guilt).

1. Fear-spending as a distraction to overcome nervousness.

2. Grief-spending to fill the void.

3. Sadness-spending to boost your mood.

4. Guilt-spending to treat yourself to overcome feelings of failure.

Do you identify with emotional spending? If yes, list the areas below.

_____
_____
_____
_____
_____
_____
_____
_____
_____
_____
_____

List 3 ways you have fallen into emotional spending.

_____
_____
_____
_____
_____
_____
_____
_____

What is one thing you can do to challenge yourself to overcome this habit?

_____

_____

_____

_____

_____

_____

_____

_____

_____

_____

_____

_____

_____

_____

_____

_____

_____

_____

_____

_____

_____

_____

_____

_____

_____

_____

_____

_____

Signs of a Compulsive Spender

Compulsive spending feels irresistible. It makes you lose all control and power to do what is rational. However, this type of continuous spending can cause personal distress, such as spending when you have little money or purchasing items that give you no joy or go unused.

Compulsive spending is a response to what is going on internally. It is the outward symptom of an internal problem. Allow me to share a few triggers that initiate compulsive spending: doubt, shame, guilt, or feelings of inadequacy. Compulsive shoppers spend with the mindset of "I got to have it." In other words, it is impulsive shopping. Impulsive reaction.

Those who identify as compulsive spenders may invest excessive time and resources to shop, similar to addiction. Compulsive spending provides temporary relief of internal turmoil by providing a temporary high or euphoria. No thought goes into spending, only a desire for that "quick fix." It's unlikely to get to the core of the internal turmoil so that you can heal, be set free from this vicious cycle which can lead to financial destruction. I challenge you to take a moment to reflect. It may be hard to do and painful but doing this can be the start of healing and taking control of your finances to promote a positive lifestyle change.

Do you identify with Compulsive Spender?

_____

_____

_____

_____

_____

_____

List at least one trigger that you can relate to.

_____

_____

_____

_____

_____

_____

_____

_____

_____

Now that you have identified at least one trigger, write, in a few sentences, what you can do to overcome these triggers.

_____

_____

_____

_____

_____

_____

_____

_____

_____

_____

_____

_____

_____

_____

_____

_____

_____

Signs of a Disciplined Spender

What is disciplined spending? Taking control of your finances by setting spending and saving goals and measuring yourself by what you achieve. It is okay to take small steps towards your financial goals. Smalls steps lead to larger steps and practice leads to mastery. Once financial discipline is established, a person can take further steps to become financially independent. Understand that discipline takes repetitive practice until mastery.

I challenge you to pay off credit card debt timely and stay focused on your financial goals. Determine your needs verses your wants. Avoid peer pressure to spend. Always check in with yourself to make sure you are on track. If you get off track, get back up and keep going. How well you can conform to your spending and savings plans is how well you achieve your financial goals.

As written in Proverbs 13:18 - He who ignores discipline comes to poverty and shame, but whoever heeds correction is honored. Do not be a shame to seek out financial wisdom to hold yourself accountable and help guide you to becoming a better manager of your money to promote a positive lifestyle change.Now practice, practice, practice until you master discipline. Take control of your money and avoid the negative spending habits as discussed in the previous chapter.

Set realistic goals, change your habits, motivate yourself to maximize your dollars (get the most of every dollar you spend), focus on budgeting, and DO NOT GIVE UP! Practice leads to discipline. Prepare to spend and have a plan for spending. Disciplined spenders are mindful while spending. Work your financial plan and your financial plan will work for you.

Do you identify with Discipline Spender? If yes, list four things that you do to be a disciplined spender.

_____

_____

_____

_____

_____

_____

_____

_____

_____

_____

_____

_____

_____

_____

_____

If you're not a disciplined spender, List at least one thing you will do to move towards financial discipline.

_____

_____

_____

_____

_____

_____

_____

_____

An example is I can win one million dollars, but if I do not have a healthy relationship with money, I will spend and have nothing to show for it. Habits don't change if the mind doesn't change or is renewed.

CHAPTER 3

BREAKING THE CYCLE OF MISHANDLING MONEY

Common Mistakes People Make with Money

Have you ever had money and then checked your bank account at the end of the week and think to yourself *where did all my money go*?

When you don't know where you spend your money, this is called mishandling your money. Mishandling money is a dangerous pattern, and it is a cycle that should be broken. Most of what we learn about money we learned in the process of growing from a child into an. As adults, we mimic what we saw in the home. If what we learned was negative, then negative is what we will do. It is important that we go through the process and do the work to break the cycle of mishandling money.

We can begin this process by changing our mindset and habits. If you want change, then change needs to start with you. Nothing changes until you change. You change when your mindset changes and your outcome changes when you change.

What small steps can you take "NOW" to change these habits for the better?

_____

_____

_____

_____

How to break the cycle!

Listed below are a few steps to take:

- Admit that what you have done in the past has now worked. Be true to yourself. Learn to live within your income and be aware of household financial habits.

- Decide to make a change. Every change starts with a decision.

- Record behavior patterns to create financial stability.

- Determine the triggers (impulse, emotions etc.). Prioritize your needs and wants.

- Choose wisely.

- Choose the best option (financing or pay cash).

- Educate yourself in financial literacy.

- Map out your spending with a budget, which is your road map to your financial destination. Creating budgets are much easier to develop than several years ago due to the available apps. Working on your budget will also help you manage your credit score. The credit score reflects how well you manage and pay your dent.

- Commit to following the road map. If you discover you have taken a wrong turn...stop...look at the map and get back on track. Do not give up! The budget is your road map the tool you use to get you to your financial destination.

- Reach out for help (Consider a financial coach, educator etc.).

Common mistakes people make with money.

- Not saving
- Paying off the wrong debt first
- Unnecessary spending
- Never-ending payments
- Living on borrowed money
- Buying a new car when a used car is more fitting for your budget.
- Spending too much on a home
- Not budgeting
- Not investing in retirement

Do you identify with any of the above mistakes? If so, what areas are you willing to begin to change?

_____

_____

_____

_____

_____

_____

_____

_____

_____

_____

_____

_____

Creating New Habits

Creating new habits can be challenging. To create new money habits, first acknowledge your current money habits are not yielding positive results or the outcome that you would like. Let's get clear about habits. In simple terms, it is a repetitive action or behavior to achieve a goal or desired outcome. A *bad habit* is a *negative* action or behavior pattern. The first step to overcoming and breaking bad habits is to be true to yourself. Every change starts with you, even breaking bad money habits. Common examples of negative money habits are procrastination, overspending, maxing out credit cards, and discretionary expenses. Discretionary expenses are non-essential expenses. They are expenses that the household can survive without.

To create healthy money habits, start with shifting your mindset. It is important that you decide and give yourself permission to replace unhealthy behavior patterns and actions with healthy ones. Also, prepare mentally, reward yourself (even for the small wins) by having a stay-at-home movie night, treat yourself with a $5 shopping spree at the Dollar store, take a day off cook a nice inexpensive meal for yourself, and avoid temptation to default into those negative habits.

Creating new money habits is a process. It is not magical, and it takes time. To help you to begin the process, I recommend the following steps to help you to create new money habits: make a budget, evaluate every purchase (want vs. need), reduce debt, buy only what you need, use cash for purchases instead of credit cards. Money experts state that a person is likely to spend less when purchasing with cash verse credit cards and debit cards. There's seems to be a thrill when swiping those cards. Each swipe stirs up a feel-good feeling.

As you think about the actions you will take to achieve your financial goal, write them out. You can start with something as small as preparing lunch at home. You don't have to implement each of these all at once but do start. Incorporate one at a time, until you become comfortable and then move to the next one. I'm reminded of the saying "insanity is doing the same thing and expecting a different result." Decide today to make a change. Change is not always easy or comfortable, but sometimes change is necessary. Implementing little habits leads to discipline.

Make a commitment! What changes will you make today?

_____

_____

_____

_____

_____

_____

_____

_____

_____

_____

List the steps that you will take to meet this goal.

_____

_____

_____

_____

_____

_____

CHAPTER 4

DEVELOPING A NEW MINDSET

Have you considered that your financial decisions and habits are influenced by our mindset? Our actions, reactions, and decisions are influenced by our beliefs. What is a mindset? Your mindset is a set of beliefs that shape how you make sense of the world and yourself. It influences how you think, feel, and behave. Essentially, it is your belief system. Past experiences, culture, education, social norms contribute to the development of your mindset. What you believe about money impacts your success or failure with money. Your money mindset is an attitude that you have about your finances. It drives how you think about money and influences how you spend and how you manage your debt. It is your core belief about money and your attitude towards it. This includes what you think you can or cannot do with money. You could be self-sabotaging yourself financially and not even know it. Fear, self-limiting beliefs, negative emotions about money can block your financial success. You will be making choices that are not in your best interest. If you feel trapped in a negative financial cycle and can't seem to get out, consider developing a new mindset.

Developing a new mindset starts with a decision and permission from yourself to engage in a new or better way of doing something. Being open to new information and embracing change. Developing a new mindset may feel uncomfortable, overwhelming, and sometimes frustrating because change is not always easy. Developing a new mindset may require letting go of limiting beliefs and behaviors. Letting go is a process.

You will need to be intentional and focus on your thoughts, actions, and behavior. Doing this will help you understand your thoughts and emotions surrounding negative money habits. Be mindful at all times so that you do not default back to what is familiar and comfortable. It's interesting that we get stuck in continuing negative patterns and behaviors that are not reaping any rewards, yet we do not want to change. It's easier to hold onto what is familiar and comfortable than to change. Change is inevitable if you intend to grow. Change is inevitable if you want a different outcome with your finances.

Developing a new mindset requires action, discipline, and commitment to the process. It often requires new information; I like to refer to this change as mental transformation. To release the old (habits, practices, and patterns) requires you to do the required work. Give yourself permission to move forward in a new way.

Without a changed mindset, it doesn't matter what you do, how much you prepare, how much you earn, win, or inherit. If you are not prepared to manage your finances, then you risk the chance of losing it all. For example, a person who wins the lottery and suddenly has no money, we wonder how this happened. How did they end up financially depleted? They did not do the work to change their mindset so that new money habits and behaviors could be developed to effectively manage money and have a new relationship with money.

Steps to developing a new mindset.

1. **Focus on learning:** Seek out reliable sources of information and focus on learning. Read books, industry publications, and quality blogs. Listen to podcasts and attend conferences. There is a lot of information out there, so work on developing the skill of identifying the best and avoiding the rest.

2. **Challenge your current beliefs:** One of the most critical steps in changing your mindset is acknowledging that you have a fixed mindset, at least in some areas. Look at your current belief system and identify where you have self-limiting beliefs. Acknowledging this isn't shameful, it's human. Shine a light on the roadblocks you're putting up for yourself and work on turning them around.

3. **Set a vision and define goals**: Creating a vision and setting goals can help provide the motivation you need to move from a fixed mindset to a growth mindset. What do you want to achieve in the next year? Five years? Ten years? Get a clear picture of where you want to be and then break your vision down into goals that will help you reach it.

4. **See failures as opportunities:** People with a growth mindset know that failure is a necessary stop on the road to success. When faced with failure, they see it as an opportunity to change tactics or apply extra effort to improve results.

5. **Be authentic:** A growth mindset demands authenticity in how you think and act. Be true to yourself. Know

who you are and what you're all about. Acknowledge where you are and where you are going in terms of financial goals.

List three steps you will take to develop a new mindset.

_____

_____

_____

_____

_____

_____

_____

_____

_____

_____

_____

_____

CHAPTER 5

THE IMPORTANCE AND BENEFITS OF BUDGETING

Budgeting is a management tool. It is planning that prepares you for the future by giving you a way to control your finances. The primary focus of budgeting is to summarize objectives, set up a timetable for actions, and to set boundaries and limits. In simple definition, a budget is an estimation of revenues and expenses over a specified future period and is usually compiled and re-evaluated on a periodic basis. Budgeting provides a simple snapshot and roadmap of the flow of your household income and expenses.

Budgeting is a topic that most of us do not like to talk about or live by. There may be many reasons that someone may choose not to budget. I agree that writing down all the money that goes towards expenses and realizing there is not enough cash can be very scary and overwhelming. As a result, many people will forgo creating a budget and simply hope that things will magically work out. It is common to feel overwhelmed when struggling financially. It's also tempting to ignore the problem with the hope that it will go away or to not deal with the reality of the situation by hoping that things will get better.

When struggling financially, the simple task of opening a bank statement or a bill can feel very overwhelming as this is a reminder of a lack of money or one more thing that needs to be paid. Stress and feelings of hopelessness can lead to feelings of despair, and this is where we find ourselves when we do not have a plan for our money. There are many apps that we use today to get us to driving destinations that we are not sure of and the same should be with finances. We know what we want, but we need a plan to get there, and that plan is a budget.

Creating a budget is all about being intentional. It helps you to create a plan to see where your money is going. When budgeting, you are telling your money where to go. A good workable budget is a budget that is simple, flexible, and helps you achieve individual or family goals.

Budgets help you to get clear view about your financial situation. Something about writing it down helps bring finances into proper perspective. One or two things will occur, you will realize that you need more money or that you need to reduce spending. You may have to get a part time job or be creative in finding ways to increase your income and stop unnecessary spending.

A good practical budget is an effective tool to use to overcome financial problems. It is your roadmap towards a financial goal. In essence, budgets allow you to see where there is unnecessary and excess spending. As you work your budget, you may need to make adjustments, which is ok. To maximize every dollar, I recommend allocating all monies to a category on the budget sheet or app.

Here are a few effects of poor budgeting or lack of budgeting: lack of savings, out of control spending, a higher likelihood of going into debt, and more financial stress. Make your budget work for you. Budgets can be adjusted as often as needed.

Budgets can be created for a person, a business, or just about anything that makes and spends money. However, it is very important to set realistic financial goals. If you're a beginner with budgeting, start small so that you don't become overwhelmed. It takes time to become comfortable with budgeting and mastering a budget. I challenge you to maximize your dollars (get the most of every dollar you spend) by creating a budget. There are many budgeting apps available online. Explore and find the right app for you or you can use a spreadsheet to create a budget. DO NOT GIVE UP!

Why do we need to budget?

Budgeting is important because it helps with perspective (helps you to see the reality of your financial situation), helps you to control spending, track expenses, and save more money. Budgeting also provides a snapshot of the household debt and brings debt into a clear view. Budgeting can also help you make better financial decisions, prepare for emergencies, get out of debt, provide guardrails (limits) for spending, peace of mind, less likely to end up in overwhelming debt and stress, and stay focused on your long-term financial goals.

In essence, budgeting brings control and order to financial chaos. As a result of taking control of your finances, managing credit also becomes less challenging. Budgeting is your individualized plan to take control of your finances to promote a positive lifestyle change. It is important to know that taking control of your finances will require you to be intentional and have a plan for getting out of debt. Budgeting will create the path for you to meet your financial goals.

Suggestion to create a budget.

1. Calculate your net income. The foundation of an effective budget is your net income.

2. Track your spending.

3. Set realistic goals.

4. Develop a plan.

5. Adjust your spending to stay on budget.

6. Review your budget regularly.

Now that you have information about budgeting. What are your thoughts about budgeting? Take a moment to answer the following questions.

1. Do you procrastinate about budgeting?

2. Do you budget?

3. Do you budget consistently?

4. Do you have fears about budgeting? If yes, what are your fears?

5. If you do budget, are you satisfied with your budget or do you need to make adjustments?

Food for thought: If large corporations, businesses, and the government create budgets, why do you think that you should not personally create a budget?

Being Smart with Money

Requires awareness and discipline. Know your strengths and weaknesses. An example of a weakness is spontaneous spending. Spontaneous spenders should plan before spending by making a list of the necessities and setting a limit as to how much you PLAN to spend. Most importantly, you must commit to the plan. People who are smart with money are aware of their finances. They create budgets and live below their means. They incorporate tools and resources into their life to help them meet their financial goals. Being smart with money also means setting specific, measurable, attainable, and realistic financial goals, and making your money work for you. Investing is a great way to make your money work for you.

As with any investment, the goal is to get a return on the money invested. Investing in yourself is also an option. Investing in yourself is to use your resources to better yourself and improve your quality of life. This could mean going back to school, taking online classes, or investing in your physical or mental health. By investing in yourself, you set aside time, effort, and resources toward activities that enhance your skills, broaden your knowledge, develop your talents and skills. What do you like to do? What are you good at doing? Do you have skills that you can use to produce an income? You can invest in yourself to learn new skills or develop your current skills to get a better job or start a business. For example, if you have skills to mow lawn, trim bushes, and design flower beds, you can take online classes to learn about properly planting grass seeds, applying mulch, and designing flower beds. Gaining knowledge and proper application technique for lawn care will help you stand out against your competitors.

Another investment option is investing in bank products. If you're not ready to invest big, then start small and invest in bank products that will give you a return. Talk with your bank representative about their investment products. Then do your research to determine which product is best for you and give you your desired outcome.

If you're ready to invest big, there are many options available such as investing in real estate, startup companies, and stocks. I do recommend that you talk with an investment advisor verse doing it on your own.

Automate when you can. This is another way to you can be smart with money. This is good for individuals who may need help paying bills timely. However, confirm the payment due date with the company so there will be no surprises. Automating bill payment will eliminate payment for late fees and also demonstrate your ability to pay bills timely. Automating Savings is another idea. Sometimes the less steps it takes to move money where it needs to be, the more likely you will stick to it.

Another smart move is to prioritize high interest debt and pay them accordingly. The sooner you pay these off the better off you will be. Pay more than the scheduled payment due whenever you are able. Paying more than the scheduled payment will help you pay off the debt sooner because more money from your payment will be applied to the principal amount. A percentage of the scheduled payment will first be applied to the interest and the remaining amount to the principal.

Consumers are constantly bombarded with special offers to make purchases with special terms. If you are going to take advantage of special offers, then I encourage you to be smart. It is important that you pay attention to the terms of the agreement and the fees associated within the terms of the agreement so that you don't get stuck paying higher cost and fees. I encourage you to never break the terms of the agreement. For example, ff you are offered 0% interest for 6 months. Make sure that you are financially able to keep these terms. Examine every offer to determine if it is right for you and the right time. Consider if you can afford it right now. Also be careful of offers that limit the repayment period. If you choose these offers, make sure you can pay it off before the offer expires to avoid being hit with interest rates or higher interest rates. Always think before you purchase. Will it benefit you or cripple you?

Smart and Practical Ways to Save:

- Be creative with savings. Turn the dread of savings into fun by exploring creative ways to save.

- 52-week challenge—Save $1 the first week, $2 second week, $3 third week. Continue to increase the amount by $1 each week for 52 weeks. You will save $1378. You can change the amount to whatever dollar amount you choose. You can use $5, $10, etc.

- No spending challenge—Challenge yourself to not spend money, except on essentials. Set a time period for the challenge such as 30 days, 60 days etc.

- No eating out for an established time frame.

- 365-day nickel saving challenge. You add a nickel to the previous day's saving every day for 365 days. For example, 1st day deposit $.05 into savings, 2nd day deposit $.10 into savings, 3rd day deposit $.15 cent into savings. At the end of 365 days, your total should be $3339.75.

These saving tips can be modified to your preference. Setting a goal for how much you want to save or how you plan to use the money will help you to stay focus.

CHAPTER 6

UNDERSTANDING CREDIT

This chapter is for those who choose to use credit. Whether or not you use credit is your decision. I believe in effectively managing finances to become debt free. However, if you choose to use credit, get an understanding so that you can make informed choices and manage credit wisely.

We'll also look at information that will help you understand credit so you can make informed decisions. Credit scores and credit history can play a critical role in an individual's ability to achieve economic security. Building your credit isn't a quick fix and it's not a one and done thing. It is a lifetime of work if you choose to use credit. Take the right steps to manage it.

Let me introduce you to the major players when it comes to credit: Equifax, Experian, Transunion, and Innovis. These are the major credit bureaus, with Innovis being the youngest of the four. These companies are a centralized source (all in one place) that houses credit data on consumers and businesses. The credit bureaus are not government agencies, but private companies. These companies maintain a credit file on you. The first day you apply for credit or a loan, is the day you begin building your file. A couple of ways the credit bureaus gather data on you each time you apply for a loan or credit. The information on your application is submitted to the bureaus. Interesting, isn't it? Lenders obtain credit information from these companies to determine an applicant's credit worthiness based on the way an applicant paid their past creditors or is paying their current creditors. In return, the creditors report their occurrences to the bureau where it is processed and added to the consumer's file.

The information reported to the bureaus is used to calculate credit scores. You have two options; you can build good credit history (high credit score) or bad credit history (low credit score)—the choice is yours. Credit scores and credit history can play a critical role in an individual's ability to achieve economic security and build wealth. Building your credit isn't a quick fix and it's not a one and done thing. It is lifetime of work if you choose to use credit. Take the right steps to manage it and you can gain access.

This number (credit score) can range from 300 to 900, with 900 being on the high end. Your credit score identifies you as either a high-risk borrower when you have a low score or a low to no risk borrower when you have a high score. In simple terms, your credit score reflects your credit worthiness. Have you considered your credit worthiness? If not, take a moment and answer these questions?

1. Are you high risk or low risk?

2. What is your credit score?

3. How often do you check your credit report?

4. Do you know that credit scores are fluid?

The credit score is fluid. As information from companies are reported to the credit bureaus, your score changes. Depending on the information reported, your score can change from good to bad.

Score Calculation

Let's identify what makes up the credit score. The FICO model has been the most common model used for scoring by lenders. This scoring system dates back to 1950 and was developed by Fair Isaac's Corporation. With the FICO model, the credit score is determined based on five categories: Past payment history, credit use, length of credit history, types of credit, and inquiries. Past payment history accounts for about 35 % of the score. Make sure you're paying your bills in a timely manner. Credit use accounts for about 30% of the score. Make sure you're not maxing out credit cards. Length of credit history accounts for about 15 % of the score. Make sure you are not closing accounts that have history and you're not opening unnecessary new accounts. Types of credit account for about 10% of the score. Finance company accounts score lower than bank or department store accounts. Inquiries account for about 10% of the score. Multiple inquiries can be a risk if several cards are applied for, or other accounts are close to maxed out. Improving your credit score will require time, effort, and discipline. As I mentioned earlier, if you choose to use credit, arm yourself with information so that you are positioned to be smart with credit and to use credit wisely. Understanding each of the five categories and mastering each category will help you to manage credit better.

Bad Credit Cost

Do you know that bad credit costs YOU money? What do you mean? I'm glad you asked. Again, whether you use credit is your choice. My goal is to share information with you so that you can make informed decisions. However, if you choose to use credit, managing it effectively is important.

You end up paying more for things like mortgages, auto loans, personal loans, and insurance, compared with those with good credit scores. You can also end up with higher payments, higher competitive interest rates, and often pay more in fees. Here's an example: A 30-year mortgage loan of $300,000 for someone with a credit score of between 760 and 850 carried a 6.346% APR. Someone with a credit score of between 500 and 850 carried a 10.152% APR. This would mean that the person with a good credit score would have a monthly payment of $1866, while the person with the poor credit score would pay $2666 which is $800 dollars more a month for the same house. That adds up to $288,000 over the 30-year loan period. I will now use an example with a credit card. Let's assume, for example, that both persons with good and bad credit carry a median credit card debt of $2,200 over 30 years. If the person with good credit had an interest rate of 9% and the person with poor credit had an interest rate of 20%, the person with poor credit will pay an extra $7,260 over 30 years. Therefore, it is imperative to do the work to get that credit score up so that you can keep as much money in your pocket as you can.

Other areas that maybe effected by credit

Other areas where credit scores may be considered are jobs. Employers may pull your credit report when you apply for a job because many see a risk in employing people with bad credit. Housing is another area. Apartment managers may run a credit check on prospective tenants. If your credit is poor, you may be denied a unit due to the risk that you may not be able to pay. Some companies may require a deposit or a larger deposit for persons with bad credit.

In addition to all the financial aspects where bad credit can hurt you, your health could be adversely affected. Knowing that you are paying more than your counterparts due to bad credit can be a stressor mentally and physically. I challenge you to take the time to make an effort to keep your credit in good standing. It will pay off with more money in your pocket and less stress in your life. Stop giving away your hard-earned money by paying higher interest rates. Stop using credit for non-essential purchases. If you MUST use credit, use credit only when the life of the purchase exceeds the payments. Now that you have a better understanding of credit you are positioned to make better choices.

List three things you will do to begin improving your score.

1.

2.

3.

Requesting Credit Reports

Everyone is entitled to obtain a free credit report at least once a year from annualcreditreport.com. Experian also provide credit reports and FICO scores, however there is a cost. Also MyFICO.com provides credit reports and FICO scores also at a cost. This is just to name a few. Pay close attention when ordering reports as you want to make sure the report includes the credit score or offers the credit score.

Soft Inquiries

There are many apps available to check your credit score. Companies have developed scoring models which have challenged the credit bureau FICO model. Scoring models can be developed from different sources of data. The credit bureau models are developed from information in the consumer credit bureau reports (the consumer's file). If you have questions as to which scoring model your lender uses, contact the lender. Checking your score in this manner is considered a soft inquiry.

CHAPTER 7

GETTING TO KNOW ASSETS AND LIABILITIES

The purpose of this section is to understand the financial terms, assets, and liabilities. There are several types of assets: business, personal, physical assets, liquid assets etc. This section is an overview of assets and liabilities. I will focus on personal assets and liabilities. My goal is to provide information that will help you to understand the difference.

What are assets and liabilities? In the most simplistic definition, assets (money in), liabilities (money out). An asset is something that contains economic value and/or future benefit. Assets can often generate cash flow. In other words, anything you can turn into money. Essentially, personal assets are things owned by an individual or household that have present or future value. Personal assets also contribute to an individual's net worth and used to grow your net worth. Your net worth is a measure of what you own minus what you owe. It is calculated by subtracting all of your liabilities from your total assets.

There are different types of personal assets. For example, Fixed Assets. Fixed Assets are things such as land, building, office furniture etc. Personal assets include things such as stocks, bonds, real estate, CDs, Savings, Money Market, Treasury Bills, personal property, land, jewelry, and collectibles. Investments are also personal assets which include but not limited to annuities, bonds, cash value of Life Insurance policy, Mutual Funds, Pensions, Retirement Plans, and stocks. Assets are a plus. Are houses considered an asset? Yes, even though most homes have a mortgage, which is a form of debt, which is a liability, the house itself is considered to be an asset as you have equity in it. Assets generate revenue. Also keep in mind that physical assets are anything tangible that you own and is of value. Liquid assets are things of value that can be converted into cash.

The opposite of money in is money out. Personal liabilities (money out) is what you owe. Assets put money in your pocket and liabilities take money out. Liabilities can hurt you. There are different types of liabilities. However, for the purpose of this, I will provide you with an overview. Examples of liability include car loan, unpaid bills, outstanding loan balances, mortgages etc. Your liabilities are everything you owe. More than likely, if your liabilities are more that your assets in terms of value, you're technically unable to pay debts owed. When liabilities exceed assets, it leads to a scenario of asset deficiency. This situation can cause financial distress because you have over borrowed and extended yourself financially. Liabilities can be short term such as credit card debt or long term such as a mortgage.

As I conclude this section, here is something you may not have considered an asset, your time, your mind, and your network. All three of these have the potential to produce revenue if you manage them wisely.

CHAPTER 8

NEGOTIATING AND USING YOUR POWER

Money is a tool used to accomplish financial goals. How you use it, can produce a positive outcome or a negative outcome. Therefore, if money is used as a tool, then why not learn how to master the tool. As it is with any tool, to master its use requires skill. A powerful tool placed in the hands of an unskilled individual can cause harm. It is no different when it comes to money. Money in the hands of an unskilled individual can also cause harm. How? Ruin your credit and have lots of debt. Taking control of your finances is one of the most powerful things you can do for yourself and your family.

Taking control of your finances and wisely managing credit (if you choose to use credit), leverages you to have more negotiating and buying power. Taking control of your finances and effectively managing credit also helps you leverage your position to negotiate when applying for credit or a loan. In some instances, you may be able to negotiate cost or competitive interest rates. Why pay more when you can pay less?

Taking control of your finances improves your self-esteem. You feel more confident. Therefore, you can have a more powerful, confident, and strategic conversation when negotiating a purchase. You don't have to feel ashamed and accept any offer presented to you when your finances are in order. Effectively managing your finances and credit allows you to be in a better position to negotiate.

What is negotiating? In simple terms, negotiating is a strategic discussion between two parties to bring about a desired outcome that both parties can agree on. People negotiate everyday whether it is negotiating a salary, contracts, or purchases.

This section is about financial negotiation. What is financial negotiation. Financial negotiation involves reaching an agreement which involves money. One example of financial negotiating is negotiating lower interest rates. Lower interest rates lead to lower overall cost of the loan. The interest rate is the amount you pay the lender for the money you borrow. This is how the lender makes money when you borrow. The higher the interest rate, the more you pay the lender for borrowing money. If the lender sees you as high risk, you will pay at a higher rate. Remember, the higher the risk, the higher the rate. This is why managing your finances and having control over your finances is important. This communicates to the lender that you are reliable, trustworthy, and dependable. Therefore, you are in a more favorable position to negotiate repayment, terms of financial agreement, and sometimes cost. Understand there is no power if your finances are not in order.

Of course, life happens and can lead to an unexpected hardship. Because of the hardship, you may need to negotiate payment amounts, balances, payment dates or request to skip a payment. You will less likely get the desired outcome if you have not managed your finances. In these instances, you may be forced to accept whatever the lender or company offers which leaves you no opportunity to negotiate. For example, you may need to negotiate with the lender of your car loan due to medical problems, unexpected debt, or unexpected family situation. If you have history of missing payments and paying late, the lender may be willing to negotiate with you. However, if you have shown to be trustworthy, reliable, and dependable as demonstrated by your payment history, the lender may be more willing to work with you. The lender may allow you to skip one or two payments without penalties.

Another example of negotiating is when purchasing a car. When purchasing a new vehicle and it is time to discuss financing, what is the first thing the company is going to do? Review your credit. As I discussed in a previous chapter, how you pay your bills, and your money behaviors and habits are reflected by your credit history. When you have been a good steward over your finances, it will reflect in your payment history and provide you leverage to negotiate. You don't have to accept whatever offer or get the highest interest. You can now maximize your advantage and take advantage of the low interest rate that is being offered and possibly not be required to have pay a deposit or downpayment. This is leverage. Leverage is when you have the ability to influence situations and people. The conversation between you and the salesman will be different than the conversation between someone whose finances are in chaos and the salesman. You will have more options verses having limited to no options.

Negotiating is a part of our daily life. Therefore, prepare so you can have the confidence needed to have a good ending.

CHAPTER 9

BIBLICAL FOUNDATION OF WEALTH

I dedicate this chapter to people who want more wealth than money! To build wealth requires a plan. A goal without a plan is just a wish. When you plan and map out your goals, it is easier to measure the results and hold yourself accountable. The topic of wealth is very broad and has many layers to it. I have attempted to highlight what I consider to be important points. In this chapter, my goal is to ignite a broader perspective of wealth. This chapter may challenge your thoughts about wealth.

First, I'll share several quotes that will enlighten you and elevate your awareness for the respect and the responsibility of money. You will also learn the power in which you have to build wealth and not just make money. As you read these quotes really hear the heart of them and the depth from which they speak. Then ask yourself; what is my response to these quotes?

If you would be wealthy, think of saving as well as getting. **—Ben Franklin**

The real measure of your wealth is how much you'd be worth if you lost all your money. **—Unknown**

He who loses money, loses much; He who loses a friend, loses much more; He who loses faith, loses all. **—Eleanor Roosevelt**

Money is multiplied in practical value depending on the number of W's you control in your life: what you do, when you do it, where you do it, and with whom you do it. **—Tim Ferriss**

Money is good for nothing unless you know the value of it by experience. —**P. T Barnum**

Never spend your money before you have earned it. —**Thomas Jefferson**

Before I share important takeaways about wealth, let's break down what is wealth because I am a Believer, and I am excited to walk in the doors of the church and talk about this chapter. I must share how I am able to gain wealth in my life and what I believe is the true order of wealth.

Proverbs 4:7 *"Wisdom is the principal thing, therefore get wisdom; and with all thy getting get understanding"*. Having wisdom is the wisest thing you can do and in whatever else you do, develop good judgement. What is wisdom? Wisdom is the ability to use knowledge in understanding basic facts, truths, and information. How to get knowledge? Knowledge is gained from education and learning. In other words, wisdom is insight to the information you have.

We must change our perspective and habits. We must level up and wear an *I am trustworthy* badge about money. Are you trustworthy? This is what Luke 16:9-11 says: *I tell you, use worldly wealth to gain friends for yourselves, so that when it is gone, you will be welcomed into eternal dwellings. 'Whoever can be trusted with very little can also be trusted with much, and whoever is dishonest with very little will also be dishonest with much. So, if you have not been trustworthy in handling worldly wealth, who will trust you with true riches?'*

1 Timothy 6:17-18 offers divine instructions for the wealthy among us. The passage reads: *Command those who are rich in this present world not to be arrogant nor to put their hope*

in wealth, which is so uncertain, but to put their hope in God, who richly provides us with everything for our enjoyment.

Just for a moment, I bring to your attention Solomon. I consider Solomon to be a smart man. When God asked Solomon, what do you want, notice that Solomon did not ask for money or material possessions, he asked for wisdom and understanding. Solomon could have asked for anything, but Solomon knew that wisdom and understanding was powerful and with it, he could build wealth.

What is wealth?

Wealth is an accumulation of resources and possessions of value. Wealth is also anything that can be handed down from generation to generation. Wealth includes adequate physical possessions to live and flourish. Society determines wealth to be an abundance of valuable possessions or money; the state of being rich with material prosperity.

It is probably safe to say that most of you reading this book have heard or maybe have been included in a conversation about wealth. When you hear the word "wealth", what do you think about? How do you define wealth? Have you considered that wealth may be more than owning luxury items? If you answered no, it's okay. Being wealthy is much deeper than these things. True wealth is about making an impact through giving, leaving a legacy, and having options for how you live your life.

Did you know that a business plan is wealth? Wealth is in the plan. As you execute the plan with wisdom and successfully, the result is riches. Riches follow wealth. An idea can be wealth. As I execute my idea and make it tangible, I can now begin to reap the benefits (wealth). What do you have in your hand that you can use to build wealth? God gives his children power (wisdom, understanding, skills, bodily strength, and health) to get wealth to confirm His covenant (Deuteronomy 8:18).

We are to be good stewards and good managers over all things.

Food for thought: If businesses and large corporations hire managers to manage operations, then why not be a good manager of your financial operations?

Being wealthy allows you to give.

Therefore, it is so important to budget. Budgeting helps you plan to spend, save, and give. How much you give is up to you. After you have taken care of your own basic needs, budgeting will help you map this out, you can also map out giving. The truth is, we are blessed to be a blessing. When your cup is full, let it overflow onto others. By working hard and building wealth, you're giving yourself an opportunity to help others around you.

Being wealthy helps you leave a legacy.

No matter your income, everyone can leave a legacy. What is a legacy? It is an amount of money or property left to someone. However, being wealthy allows you to make a bigger impact beyond yourself and your family, if you manage your wealth right. Building a legacy is about creating something that will outlive you and transform the lives of people you may never even meet.

Building Wealth vs. Getting Rich

There's an important distinction to make here: Building

wealth versus becoming rich. Becoming rich happens when you experience a financial windfall or a sudden influx of money. Here are two examples of financial windfalls: receiving an inheritance, or a pro athlete signing a deal. Hopefully, you get the idea.

Sadly, you can blow through lots of money in the blink of an eye! That's because the good habits that allow people to build wealth (generosity, planning, discipline, and consistency) are the same habits that help people maintain their wealth. I think it's safe to say that no one becomes wealthy by accident. Of course, there is the exception like individuals who receive an inheritance. However, you must set a goal to work hard, grow your money, and show up day after day to make that dream a reality.

Being wealthy is also all about our mindset and how we perceive our own well-being. Get a wealthy mindset. Most of us are money-minded and not wealth-minded so we are working for a paycheck. Do you know that money follows wealth? We look at a big house and we say that's wealth. No, that's riches. I ask you to take a moment and ponder this—who gives wisdom, understanding, skills, bodily strength, and health? Without these how can wealth be obtained?

I offer a few ways to build wealth.

- Increase your income.
- Start a business.
- Improve your skill set.
- Create a budget.
- Live below your means.

- Invest (in yourself).

- Invest (stocks, bonds, etc.).

- Be a generous and give

Importantly, get wisdom, get knowledge, and understanding. Wisdom is application, and knowledge is information and understanding is comprehension. Solomon was one of the wisest men in the Bible. He could have asked for anything, but he asked for wisdom. An individual can have knowledge and understanding but no wisdom (no application). If you don't apply what you know, it does not benefit you.

Haggai 2:7-9: *'I will shake all nations, and what is desired by all nations will come, and I will fill this house with glory,' says the Lord Almighty. 'The silver is mine and the gold is mine,' declares the Lord Almighty. 'The glory of this present house will be greater than the glory of the former house,' says the Lord Almighty. 'And in this place, I will grant peace,' declares the Lord Almighty.*

This last scripture says that God owns it all! I wanted to share this to remind us that we need order for our lives so things can flow! How do we get this order?

1. Put God first.

2. Be good stewards.

3. Become trustworthy towards money and every aspect of your life.

CONCLUSION

Being Smart with Money will challenge you to rethink how you interact with money. I believe that as you increase your awareness and knowledge about financial literacy, you will be able to make informed and effective decisions with all your financial resources. Stop the negative cycles of mismanaging money. Identify those core issues that have kept you bound in financial chaos. Then decide and an make an earnest effort to defeat debt and effectively manage your finances.

Printed in the USA
CPSIA information can be obtained
at www.ICGtesting.com
LVHW070712130624
783027LV00018B/183

9 781964 234076